9601441
LGAA

HISTORY

MAKERS of

the SECOND

WORLD WAR

ILLUSTRATED BY

JESSICA CURTIS

HISTORY MAKERS

First published in 1995 by
Wayland (Publishers) Ltd
61 Western Road, Hove,
East Sussex BN3 1JD,
England

© Copyright 1995 Wayland (Publishers) Ltd

Series editor: Katie Roden
Series designer: Tracy Gross
Book designer: Joyce Chester

British Library Cataloguing in Publication Data

Gilbert, Adrian
Second World War. – (History Makers Series)
I. Title   II. Curtis, Jessica   III. Series
940.54

ISBN 0 7502 1269 1

Typeset by Dorchester Typesetting Group Ltd,
England
Printed and bound in Italy by Lego

Notes for teachers

History Makers uses a wide range of exciting contemporary sources – quotations, letters, paintings, photographs and artefacts – to build up detailed and informative portraits of people who made important contributions both to their own time and to the way we live now.

This book:

- features important figures from all areas of life during the Second World War – the military, the home front, science, the arts and government;

- presents contemporary reactions to changes and innovations;

- focuses on the long-term and short-term effects of the Second World War on all levels of society;

- emphasizes the importance of the era for modern life.

Picture acknowledgements:

Associated Press 18, 30, 33 (bottom); Bridgeman Art Library 11, 13 (bottom); Mary Evans Picture Library 39 (left); Hulton Deutsch 10, 26, 37, 41, 42; Imperial War Museum 6, 7, 8 (bottom), 9 (top), 12, 13 (top), 15, 16, 17 (both), 19 (both), 20, 21, 22 (bottom), 23, 29, 31, 32, 36 (top left), 40; Keystone Press Agency 33 (top); London Express News Service 27 (right); Popperfoto 8 (top), 9 (bottom), 22 (top), 24, 28, 35 (both), 36 (top right, bottom), 38; Topham Picture Source 39 (right), 43 (both); Wayland Picture Library 14, 25 (both, © Solo Syndication/ Evening Standard/Centre for Study of Cartoons and Caricature, University of Kent at Canterbury), 27 (left).

C o n t e n t s

Words in **bold** in the text are explained in the Glossary on page 44.

Winston Churchill

1874 – 1965

'At last I had the authority to give directions over the whole scene. I felt as if I was walking with destiny, and that all my past life had been but a preparation for this hour and for this trial.'

Churchill wrote these words on the night after he was made Prime Minister on 10 May 1940. For the next five years he would be the leader of a country at war, fighting an intense battle for survival against the threat of **Nazi Germany**.

The outbreak of war against Germany in 1939 is announced at a news-stand in London. The war gave Winston Churchill the opportunity to prove his ability as a leader.

6

Winston Churchill was born into a rich and powerful family. As a young man he was a soldier and a journalist before he entered politics. Although he quickly became a high-ranking politician in the **Conservative Party**, many people did not trust him because he would often change his views on an important matter to suit himself.

Over a long period, he was appointed and then sacked from many of the most important jobs in politics. By 1929, it seemed that his career was over. But when war was declared ten years later, Churchill came back into favour again because it was thought that he would make a good Prime Minister in wartime.

When he became Prime Minister, Britain was in terrible trouble. The British army had been defeated by the Germans in France and Belgium, and it seemed possible that the Germans might invade Britain. While some politicians wanted to surrender and make peace, Churchill was determined that Britain would fight on until Germany was defeated. He made many inspiring speeches on the radio. One of his finest speeches to the nation ended:

'... we shall fight on the beaches, we shall fight on the landing grounds, we shall fight in the fields and in the streets, we shall fight in the hills; we shall never surrender.'

Churchill talks to British soldiers during the war. His rousing speeches encouraged the troops to fight harder.

OTHER WAR LEADERS

President Franklin D. Roosevelt (1882–1945) – US President 1933–45. General Charles de Gaulle (1890–1970) – a French general and statesman. Head of the French government 1944–6 and President of France 1959–69. Joseph Stalin (1879–1953) – Soviet leader 1924–53. Adolf Hitler (see pages 16–20)

The devastating effect of the war can be seen in this picture of a bombed London street. Churchill encouraged people not to give up hope and to work as hard as they could for the war effort.

Churchill worked very hard to increase Britain's fighting strength. He brought in special people, such as new ministers and advisers, to help improve the **war effort**. In 1940, the German air force was defeated by the RAF in the Battle of Britain, and Britain was saved from the possibility of a German invasion.

Churchill visits a British anti-aircraft battery during the summer of 1940.

The British were very short of weapons and equipment, so Churchill persuaded the US President, Franklin D. Roosevelt, to send supplies from the USA. Eventually, the USA joined Britain in the war, after the Japanese attack on **Pearl Harbor**.

Churchill liked to be involved with military operations. This used to annoy his generals who often felt that the Prime Minister was getting in the way. Sometimes Churchill would have big arguments with his commanders, and on several occasions he had them sacked. One soldier wrote:

'Winston was an excellent chap but he was always pestering our generals to do this or do that. His schemes could be hare-brained at times, and this made life very uncomfortable for the commanders in the front line.'

At the end of the war a **general election** was called, and Churchill lost his job as Prime Minister. The people knew he was a good war leader but they wanted a different type of government in peacetime. Although Churchill became Prime Minister again during the 1950s, it was the years between 1940 and 1945 that were important, when his courageous actions made him one of the great history makers of the Second World War.

Churchill meets General Montgomery, a British field marshal, at his headquarters in France in 1944. Churchill always took a direct interest in the fighting, and often disagreed with his generals.

HOT SEAT

This cartoon by David Low shows Churchill returning to the 'hot seat' when he became Prime Minister for the second time in 1951.

9

Laura Knight
1877–1970

'I was given no particular subject to paint, and after a week or two spent looking around, I chose "Take-Off". I studied the actual look of the crew at this moment from inside the plane itself before its evening visit to Berlin. I learnt that there were two moments when the crew of a loaded bomber knew fear – before going down the runway at take-off and when over the target.'

Laura Knight hard at work. She made many sketches before she began a painting.

Laura Knight was an artist who painted many pictures during the Second World War. One of her most famous was *Take-Off*, which shows the crew of a bomber aircraft just at the point when it takes to the air.

Called *Take-Off*, this famous painting shows the crew of a bomber aircraft just before leaving on a mission.

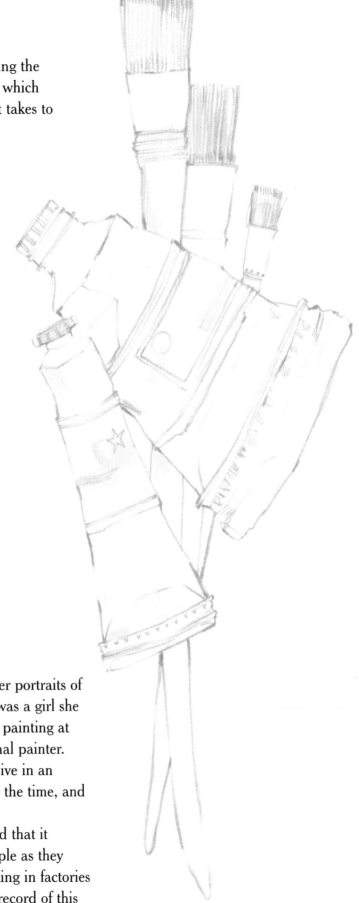

Before the war, Knight had become well known for her portraits of travellers, ballet dancers and circus people. Ever since she was a girl she had wanted to be an artist, and because she was so good at painting at school she had gone to art college to train to be a professional painter. After marrying another student at the college, she went to live in an artists' colony in Cornwall, England. There she painted all the time, and soon had a good reputation as an artist.

When the war started, the British government decided that it wanted the country's artists to paint pictures of British people as they went about their work, whether in the armed forces or working in factories and offices. The government wanted to leave a permanent record of this very important time in Britain's history. Laura Knight was one of the artists chosen to do this job.

As an Official War Artist, Knight painted a series of pictures of WAAFs (Women's Auxiliary Air Force members), who helped the RAF with its work. One of the best known of these pictures was called *In for Repairs*, a painting of a **barrage balloon** being repaired by WAAFs. After finishing it she wrote to the WAAF commanding officer:

'The balloon posed like a great silver toad with a pulse in its side, due I suppose to the draught coming from the door. I saw lots of other subjects there good enough to paint, particularly the girls in battledress going through training...'

WAAFs work on a bomber aircraft, cleaning the engines and repairing the wings. Women played an important part in the British war effort, a fact recorded by Laura Knight.

DATE CHART

1877
Born in Nottingham, England as Laura Johnson.

1903
Marries portrait painter Harold Knight.

1929
Made a Dame of the British Empire (DBE) for her services to painting.

1945
Travels to Nuremberg in Germany to paint Nazi war criminals.

1945–70
Works as an artist, specializing in portraits.

1970
Dies at the age of ninety-three.

One of her most important commissions was to paint a young woman called Ruby Lofthouse, who worked in a factory making guns. She was especially good at her job, having learned how to do it in two years when most people took twice that time. Knight went down to the factory and made many sketches of Ruby at work. While she was sketching one day, a loose wheel came crashing down, but instead of ducking out of the way, Knight threw herself over her drawing to protect it from damage. Her art was more important than her own safety!

At the end of the war, Laura Knight was asked to travel to Nuremberg in Germany to produce a painting at the trial of the most brutal Nazi war criminals. She found it a fascinating experience, drawing pictures of some of the most powerful Germans who had ruled much of Europe during the previous five years. Once they had the power of life or death over millions of people, but now they were on trial for *their* lives.

Ruby Lofthouse Screwing a Breech Ring by Laura Knight. This picture is a good example of Knight's wartime painting, showing the important work done by women during the war.

After the war she continued to paint, mainly as a portrait artist. Laura Knight is remembered for realistic and exciting pictures of all kinds of subjects; many art critics think that her wartime paintings were among the best she produced.

Knight was very interested in painting dancers and people involved in the theatre. *Dressing Room at Drury Lane* shows ballet dancers about to go on stage.

Albert Einstein

1879-1955

'Are they crazy, or am I?'

Albert Einstein is considered to be one of the greatest scientists of the twentieth century. His theories are extremely complicated, and even today many people, including leading scientists, find them very hard to understand.

Although Einstein was born in Germany, he moved to Zurich, in Switzerland, as a young man. He was devoted to science, especially **physics**, but he was short of money so he had to take a clerical job. After work, however, he would go to local cafes and try to prove his theories in front of the other customers – theories that eventually would transform modern science.

Albert Einstein (centre) prepares to give a lecture on his *Theory of Relativity*. Einstein was the most famous scientist of the twentieth century, changing the way people thought about time, space and solid objects.

Einstein's first major work was his *Special Theory of Relativity*, which discussed time and movement in a completely new way. This was followed by his *General Theory of Relativity*, which quickly established him as a leading scientist. He was made a professor of physics at Berlin University, Germany.

A Nazi soldier rounds up opponents of Hitler. Because he was Jewish, Einstein was forced to leave Germany and continue his career in the USA.

However, in 1933 the Nazis came to power in Germany, and because Einstein was Jewish he was sacked from his job. He moved to the USA, where he continued to work as a scientist. He also wrote about the plight of the hundreds of Jewish refugees who had fled from Germany to the USA. In 1939 he wrote to the US President, Franklin D. Roosevelt, to warn him of the dangers of the **atomic bomb**, which he knew the Nazis were trying to produce. As a result, the **Allies** speeded up the work on their bomb, even though Einstein tried to persuade the US government that atomic bombs should never be used.

Einstein did not like the way countries boasted about the cleverness of their scientists. He once wrote:

'If my theory of relativity is proved successful, Germany will claim me as a German and France will declare me as a citizen of the whole world. Should my theory prove untrue, France will say I am a German, and Germany will say I am a Jew.'

DATE CHART

1879
Einstein is born in Ulm, southern Germany.

1896–1900
Studies physics and maths at the Federal Polytechnic Academy, Zurich, Switzerland.

1903
Marries Mileva Maric.

1905
Publishes his *Special Theory of Relativity*.

1913–33
Is a professor of physics at Berlin University.

1916
Publishes his *General Theory of Relativity*.

1933
The Nazis come to power in Germany. Einstein flees to the USA.

1939
Warns President Roosevelt of the dangers of Germany leading the race to make an atomic bomb.

1945
US atomic bombs are dropped on Hiroshima and Nagasaki, Japan.

1955
Dies in the USA.

OTHER SCIENTISTS

Alan Turing (1912–54) – a British scientist who developed early computers and code-cracking equipment.

A d o l f   H i t l e r

1 8 8 9 - 1 9 4 5

'I first met Hitler in 1931. His voice impressed me. I felt, "Here is a man who thinks not of himself, but of Germany!"'

These words were spoken by a young German woman. Hitler's strong personality and powerful speeches had a similar effect on many people, and this helps to explain why he was so successful in getting to the top in German politics.

Not everyone was so impressed, however. One British writer remembers trying to interview the German leader:

'He suddenly started shouting … and while he was shouting I am convinced that I could have walked out of the room and he would not have noticed my departure.'

The German leader in mid-speech. Although to some people, Adolf Hitler just seemed to rant and rave, many others were inspired by his speeches.

Born in Austria, Hitler moved to Germany when he was a young man, and fought in the German army during the First World War (1914–18). The German defeat in 1918 came as a great shock to Hitler, which he was determined to avenge. After the war he entered politics, and soon became the leader of the extreme, **right-wing** National Socialist (Nazi) Party.

The young Hitler (above) joins the crowd to welcome the outbreak of the First World War in 1914.

The entrance to Dachau Concentration Camp, where thousands of the people who had been imprisoned by the Nazis were murdered.

The Nazis were given money by rich **industrialists** and other supporters in Germany. At the time, the country's economy was in a terrible state, and Hitler promised the German people richness and power. His message was very popular with the people, and in 1933 he was made Chancellor (the head of the German government).

OTHER NAZI LEADERS

Hermann Göring (1893–1946) – a field marshal and commander who founded the Gestapo, the brutal state police.
Paul Goebbels (1897–1945) – Hitler's minister of propaganda.
Rudolf Hess (1894–1987) – a leader who later served life imprisonment for his crimes during the war.

Hitler addresses the crowd at a rally in Nuremberg in 1935. The Nazis deliberately staged these great spectacles to impress the German people with their strength and power.

Hitler made Germany a **dictatorship**, with all power concentrated within the Nazi Party. Anyone who disagreed with the Nazis was treated harshly. Hitler also turned upon Germany's large Jewish population. Jewish people were prevented from working and were later sent in great numbers to **concentration camps**, where millions of them were murdered.

Having gained control of Germany, Hitler started his campaign to rule Europe, invading Austria and parts of Czechoslovakia. In 1939, he ordered the invasion of Poland. This sparked off the Second World War, when France and Britain declared war on Hitler's Nazi Germany in order to defend Poland.

At first, the German armies were incredibly successful. They swiftly conquered Poland, and the following year invaded France. By the end of 1940, Hitler practically ruled Europe, and his dream of total European domination seemed to be coming true. However, in 1941 he tried to invade the former **Soviet Union**. The Soviet army fought back and the Germans lost many troops. At the same time, the USA joined the war on the Allied side, bringing a great deal more money and troops to use against Hitler and so enabling the Allies to be a much more powerful force.

In 1944, while the Soviet army drove the Germans out of Russia, an Anglo-American army invaded northern France. The Allies gradually advanced on the capital of Germany, Berlin, where Hitler had his headquarters. Even though Germany was now weak, Hitler still hoped he would be able to prevent defeat. As Soviet troops fought their way into Berlin, however, Hitler finally realized he had lost. Unable to cope with defeat, he shot himself.

Hitler's ambition and greed for power had brought Germany to ruin, but before he committed suicide he condemned his country in these final words:

'The German people have not shown themselves worthy of their Führer (leader), and he can only die.'

The end is in sight for Hitler's dreams of a Nazi empire (above). German soldiers are led away by Allied troops during the recapture of Paris in 1944.

After liberating a concentration camp, American soldiers look in horror at dead prisoners – victims of Hitler's policies. The prisoners have been beaten, starved and tortured.

DATE CHART

1889
20 April: Hitler is born in Brunau, Austria, the son of a customs official.

1914–18
Enlists in the German army and is awarded the Iron Cross for bravery.

1921
Becomes president of the Nazi Party.

1933
30 January: Hitler is named Chancellor, and the Nazis become the main political party in Germany.

1939
1 September: Germany invades Poland. The Second World War begins.

1944
20 July: There is a failed attempt to assassinate Hitler, by senior German officers who want to end the war.

1945
30 April: Russian troops capture Berlin. Hitler commits suicide.

Dwight D. Eisenhower

1890 - 1969

'He had the gift of making you feel you were more important than he was himself.'

Eisenhower was one of the leading generals on the Allied side during the Second World War. He commanded the armies of the USA and Britain in the great invasion of Europe in 1944, which led to the destruction of Hitler and Nazi Germany. Eisenhower was a very patient man, who was good at getting on with people – qualities which were very important in a war leader.

General Dwight D. Eisenhower talks to US airborne troops just before the invasion of Europe in June 1944. Eisenhower was good at getting on with his troops, whether they were generals or ordinary soldiers.

Raised in Kansas, USA, Eisenhower decided on an army career and graduated from the military college at West Point in 1915. He rose slowly in rank until 1935, when he joined the staff of General Douglas Macarthur in the Philippines. Macarthur liked the young staff officer and encouraged his progress.

In 1941, the USA entered the war against Japan and Germany. Talented officers were needed for this huge operation, and in 1942 Eisenhower was made Commander in Chief of the US forces in Europe. He was put in charge of the US amphibious landings (using vehicles that could travel on both land and water) in North Africa.

US troops operate a machine-gun during the Battle of the Bulge, 1944, when German forces pushed the Allied troops back into Belgium from France.

Eisenhower's time in Africa was a good preparation for his next task, to lead the Anglo-American invasion of Europe in June 1944. As **Supreme Allied Commander**, he had to make sure that all his generals would work well together. This was often a very difficult task – in his diary he wrote of the frequent tensions between the British general Bernard Montgomery, also known as 'Monty', and the US general George Patton:

'George has no love of the British in general and Monty in particular. They're like oil and water to each other. Monty has lofty ideas about US "inexperience".'

OTHER COMMANDERS

Erwin Rommel (1891–1944) – the 'Desert Fox'. A German field marshal.
George S. Patton (1885–1945) – a US general who held command during the war.
William Slim (1891–1970) – a British field marshal, and later governor-general of Australia.
Bernard Montgomery (1887–1976) – a British field marshal, who commanded the ground forces during the Normandy landings.

Eisenhower (centre), surrounded by the senior Allied commanders responsible for the invasion of Europe. Eisenhower's special strength was in bringing together officers from the armies, the navies and the air forces of different countries, to form one strong, effective fighting force.

However, Eisenhower was able to get the two men to accept his leadership, and to work together effectively. The British **Chief of Staff**, General Sir Alan Brooke, knew Eisenhower well and, although he did not think he was a very good battlefield commander, he was full of praise for his other skills in leadership:

'A past-master in the handling of allies, entirely impartial and consequently trusted by all. A charming personality and a good co-ordinator.'

The 1944 **D-Day** landings by the Allied forces in Normandy, France, which were led by Eisenhower, were a great success, and after two months of hard, bloody fighting the German army was finally driven out of France.

British troops disembark on the Normandy beaches on D-Day, 6 June 1944. Success in this battle gave the Allies a way into Europe.

A French child waves the US flag as the Allied troops arrive in Normandy on D-Day, 1944.

DATE CHART

1890
14 October: Eisenhower is born in Denison, Texas. His family soon moves to Kansas.

1915
Graduates from West Point military academy as a second lieutenant.

1939
The Second World War begins.

1941
7 December: USA enters the war after an attack on the US naval base at Pearl Harbor, Hawaii.

1942
November: US landings in North Africa, led by Eisenhower.

1944
6 June: D-Day. The Allied invasion of north-west Europe begins. The landings are successful.

1945
7 May: Eisenhower accepts the unconditional German surrender.

1952
Eisenhower is elected US President.

1956
Is elected for a second term.

1969
Dies at his home.

Although the war in Europe continued into 1945, it was soon obvious that the Allies would eventually win. On 7 May 1945, Eisenhower accepted the German **surrender** at his headquarters in Rheims, France.

After the war, Eisenhower was asked to stay in the army and was given the top job of Chief of Staff. He was later made commander of **NATO**, which had been set up to defend Europe from any possible threat from the former Soviet Union.

Eisenhower retired from the army in 1945. He was chosen to be the presidential candidate of the Republican Party in the 1952 US elections. He won and became President, and was re-elected in 1956. Although he was a successful President, Eisenhower will be best remembered as an important war leader, one who understood how to encourage and support his troops.

David Low

1891 – 1963

'The physical conditions for cartooning during the blasting of London were discouraging. I would rise exhausted from sleep in our one "fortified" room (sandbags, beams and sheet iron) huddled with the other nine members of my household. I would walk, side-stepping the bomb holes, to my studio.'

This is David Low's description of life during the Blitz in 1940–41, when German bombers attacked London and other British cities. By 1940, Low was the country's most important political cartoonist – a person who draws pictures of politicians, usually to make fun of them and their policies.

The cartoonist David Low is seen here with some of his work. The man with the hat is a self-portrait, drawn when Low had a beard, while the man flying above Low's head is his famous Colonel Blimp character.

24

This cartoon shows Hitler (with a gun) and Göring (with a spear) turning on the German people. The Nazi salute consisted of one hand raised in the air, but the Nazis have made the people 'salute with both hands now' – in an act of surrender!

David Low was born in New Zealand, and from an early age he was very good at drawing funny pictures of people he knew. This talent was spotted by a local newspaper, and soon he was making a living producing cartoons for the paper. After a short time working in Australia, Low came to Britain and became a top cartoonist.

In 1927 he joined the *Evening Standard* newspaper, which was then owned by Lord Beaverbrook. The two men became friends, despite the fact that they disagreed about politics. Before the war, Beaverbrook wanted Britain to be friendly towards Adolf Hitler, the **dictator** of Germany, and to Italy's dictator, Benito Mussolini. Low hated both men, and drew many cartoons poking fun at their activities. Although Beaverbrook did not like the cartoons, he let them appear in his papers because he thought Low was an excellent artist.

A cartoon showing the 'reception committee' facing the Nazis if they tried to invade Britain. It would not be very friendly, as the British troops would be joined by soldiers from New Zealand, Canada and Australia, all determined to destroy the Nazis.

25

Hermann Göring was a top Nazi and commander of the German air force. Low enjoyed drawing Göring, because of his large size and brutal appearance.

OTHER WAR CARTOONISTS

Ronald Searle (b.1920) – a satirist. Captured by the Japanese during the war. 'Pont' (the pen name of Graham Laidler) Philip Zec Rowland Emett

The German and Italian governments so hated Low's cartoons that they had the newspapers he worked for banned in their countries. They even tried to make the British government stop Low, but he carried on as usual. He drew a series of cartoons about a silly man called 'Muzzler', who was a combination of Mussolini and Hitler.

Another famous character invented by Low was called Colonel Blimp. He was an old soldier who said idiotic things. Some people thought Low was making fun of the British army, but all he was trying to do was to show how people often come out with stupid sayings without thinking first.

During the war, Low's cartoons were greatly enjoyed by the people of Britain, and they had a strong influence on the way people thought about politics and the war. He could produce a drawing that summed up what people were thinking at the time. Sometimes it was difficult to produce a cartoon almost every day, yet he always managed to come up with something funny and clever.

In 1945 Low was asked to attend the **Nuremberg trials** (like Laura Knight) and record the event with his cartoons. The two most important Nazi criminals were Hermann Göring and Rudolph Hess. Low described the experience of seeing them:

A caricature by Low of Lord Beaverbrook (above), a publisher who was made Minister for Aircraft Production during the war.

'Sketchbook in hand, I am examining Göring meticulously when he turns his gaze and hooks my eye. After about two minutes of mutual glaring it dawns upon me that he is trying to stare me down. How silly! (I win by the way.)
The appearance of Hess takes me aback. Down to skin and bone, going bald, wild eyes set in deep-sunken cavities, he has a nervous twitch and jerky movements. If, as he now insists, he is not mad, all I can say is that he looks it.'

After the war, David Low carried on his work as a political cartoonist. He left the *Evening Standard* and worked for other newspapers until his retirement. His cartoons are a fascinating record of the era of the Second World War.

Amy Johnson

1903 – 41

'Long-distance flyers always "cop-it". I know where I shall finish up – in the drink.'

Amy Johnson became very famous before the war as a pioneer of long-distance flying. She flew over 19,000 kilometres from Britain to Australia in a tiny plane, at a time when a flight of more than 150 kilometres was considered daring by most people. She always knew that flying could be very dangerous, and thought that one day she would crash into the sea, or 'the drink' as she called it.

Amy Johnson, one of the great pioneers of long-distance flight, climbs out of her aircraft.

When war was declared, Johnson wanted to join the RAF as a fighter pilot. She was a superb flyer. In fact, she had more flying experience than almost all the regular RAF pilots, but because she was a woman she could only join the Air Transport Auxiliary (ATA). The ATA was responsible for flying new aircraft from the factories to the airfields. This was important work because new aircraft were needed throughout the war, but female pilots were paid less than men.

Johnson thought this was unfair. She wrote to her parents:

'I'm trying to work up an agitation about the women getting equal pay for equal work. It's a question of principle.'

Early in January 1941, Johnson set out to fly an aircraft from Scotland to the south of England. Tragically, something went wrong and the plane crashed into the sea at the mouth of the River Thames, where she drowned in the cold water. Sadly, her prediction had come true – she finished up 'in the drink'. Nevertheless, Amy Johnson proved to the world that women could be just as good pilots as men.

Women pilots of the ATA meet up after flying their aircraft to front-line airfields during the war. The ATA played a very important role in the war effort, flying newly built aircraft from factories to airfields, a job that was often very dangerous.

DATE CHART

1903
Born in England.

1928
Begins flying.

1930
Flies solo from London to Darwin, Australia.

1940
Joins ATA as a ferry pilot.

1941
7 January: crashes into the sea and drowns.

OTHER EARLY LONG-DISTANCE PILOTS

Amelia Earhart (1898–1937) – the first woman to fly solo over the Atlantic Ocean.
Charles Lindbergh (1902–74) – made the first non-stop solo flight over the Atlantic.
John Alcock (1892–1919) and **Arthur Brown (1886–1948)** – the first people to fly over the Atlantic.

O s k a r   S c h i n d l e r

1908 – 74

'In the years 1941 and '42 there was plenty of public evidence of people behaving like pigs. The Jews were being destroyed. I had to help them, there was no choice.'

During the time when Hitler ruled Germany (1933–45), the Nazis ruthlessly **persecuted** Jewish people. Few people were brave enough to try to stop them, but Oskar Schindler was one person who did.

Oskar Schindler in 1957, standing in a street in the USA which has been named after him.

30

Dressed in their striped uniforms, Jewish
concentration camp prisoners are led to work.
The conditions in the camps were terrible, but few
people were brave enough to defy the Nazis and
save the prisoners.

Schindler was a businessman before the war, but he was not very
successful and spent much of his time and money on drinking and
gambling. When Poland was conquered by the Germans, Schindler
decided that he might be able to make more money by setting up a
business there. It was in Poland that Schindler first saw Jewish people
being used as **slave labour** by the Nazis.

Schindler bought a factory which made equipment for the
German army, and he employed hundreds of Jewish workers from the
city of Krakow. He still had an extravagant lifestyle: he kept expensive
race horses, for example, which he would exercise by riding them around
the factory. He made many friends among the leading Nazi officers in
the area.

However, the reality of the Nazis' treatment of the Jews gradually
affected Schindler, and he began to have a change of heart, as described
by one Jewish survivor:

*'He was a German, he wore the Nazi insignia, but when he was
out on his horse he saw what was happening in the camp and it
changed him.'*

The human cost of the Nazi campaign – dead and dying prisoners in a concentration camp. Schindler risked his life to save the camp inmates.

Revolted by the behaviour of his fellow Nazis, Schindler began to look after his Jewish workers. He gave them extra food and medicines, and he stopped them from being sent to the Nazi concentration camp at Auschwitz. He still had to keep the leading Nazis happy, however, and he would regularly **bribe** them with expensive luxuries and lavish entertainments so that they thought he was loyal to them. He even sold his wife's jewellery to raise more money. When his Nazi bosses asked him why he was not sending Jews to the concentration camps, Schindler would say angrily:

'Stop killing my workers. We've got a war to win.'

As Germany began to lose the war and the Soviet Red Army got near the camps, the Nazis killed any remaining Jews. In order to save his workers, Schindler smuggled out 1,100 of them to a place of safety in Czechoslovakia. When the fighting ended, surviving Jews came forward to tell the Allies of his good work, so that he would not be punished as a war criminal.

32

The Nazis persecuted anyone who helped or was even friends with Jewish people. This woman has been forced to wear a placard saying 'I am the greatest swine in town and only mix with Jews'.

After the war, Schindler carried on his business activities, and was helped by a Jewish relief organization to begin a new enterprise in Argentina. But this scheme failed, and he was no more successful when he returned to Germany in 1957. After the failure of a cement-making factory, Schindler spent the rest of his life alone in a small flat in the city of Frankfurt.

To Jewish people around the world, Schindler's actions were not forgotten. One of his former workers wrote:

'Schindler was like a little Noah. Getting into his camp was paradise for us. There were other German factory owners who kept Jews from the death camps for a time, but only Schindler kept his promise to save us, only Schindler stayed true.'

Schindler at a Remembrance Day service in Jerusalem, 1962, surrounded by some of the Jewish people he helped to save.

OTHERS TO STUDY

Anne Frank (1929–45) – a Jewish girl whose diaries tell how her family hid from the Nazis in Amsterdam in the Netherlands.

Leonard Cheshire

1917 - 92

*'His personal contribution to the **morale** and efficiency of Bomber Command was remarkable. By his own example he certainly succeeded in a short space of time in raising the normal standards of courage and risk-taking.'*

The task of Bomber Command was to fly over Germany and **occupied Europe** and bomb important targets on the ground. Leonard Cheshire showed that he was one of the best and bravest pilots on the British side.

Cheshire learned to fly while he was at university, and when war broke out in 1939 he immediately joined the Royal Air Force (RAF). After training he was sent to fly bomber aircraft.

This was a very dangerous job, as the slow-moving bombers of the RAF were easily shot down by German fighter planes and anti-aircraft guns. But Cheshire was a naturally gifted pilot and he was able to dodge out of the way of attacking planes. Soon he was promoted to command a **squadron** of bomber aircraft.

One of the top units in the RAF was 617 Squadron, which was used for special and dangerous missions. Every good pilot wanted to join 617 Squadron, and Cheshire was delighted when he was made squadron leader in 1943.

Instead of flying the big Lancaster bombers used by the rest of 617 Squadron, Cheshire would often fly a smaller and faster Mosquito or Mustang plane. This would help him to get to the target quickly, from where he could direct the other British aircraft safely to the right place.

Cheshire flew over 100 dangerous missions, and as a reward for his courage and skill he was awarded the Victoria Cross, Britain's highest award for bravery.

34

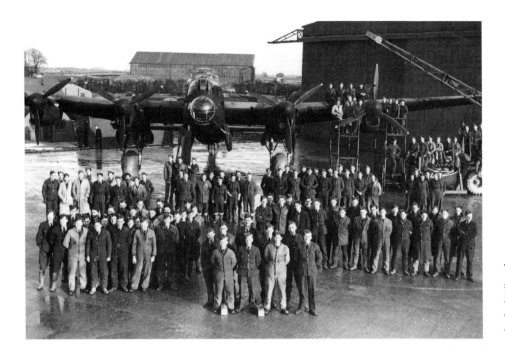

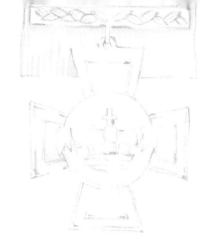

The crews of an RAF bomber squadron stand in front of a Lancaster bomber aircraft. The four-engined Lancaster was capable of carrying heavy loads of bombs deep into occupied Europe.

As well as looking after the air crew who flew the bombing missions, Cheshire always had a kind word for the people who worked in the offices, repair sheds and cookhouses of 617 Squadron. These men and women were often forgotten by powerful people during the war, but Cheshire made sure that they felt as important as the pilots. One man who helped to repair the bombers said:

'I was proud to belong to the squadron, not because of what Cheshire did but because of what he was. It was nice to feel all the time that we had a human being for a boss, someone who appreciated our work. I don't think I've ever worked harder in my life than when I worked for Cheshire. And I can't remember a happier period in the RAF.'

Leonard Cheshire used the fast, versatile Mosquito bomber aircraft to guide the slower Lancasters to their targets.

OTHER RAF BOMBER PILOTS

Guy Gibson
– a Wing Commander.
John Nettleton
– a squadron leader.
Donald Bennett
– an Air Vice-Marshal.

The power of the atomic bomb can be seen in this photograph (left) of the mushroom cloud from the huge explosion at Nagasaki.

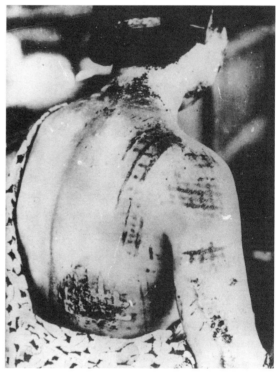

The human cost of the atomic bomb is shown by this picture of a woman's back (above). The pattern of her kimono has been burnt into her skin by the heat of the blast.

The view on the ground (left) following the atomic bomb attack on Nagasaki. The whole town was completely destroyed.

Because of his great experience as a bomber pilot, Cheshire was chosen to be one of the British official observers of the US atomic bomb raid on the Japanese city of Nagasaki. The bomb exploded successfully and helped to force Japan to surrender to the USA and Britain. But thousands of innocent people were killed, including women and children who had nothing to do with the war.

All the pain and horror caused by the war, including Nagasaki and the bombing of German cities by the RAF, made Cheshire decide to start a new, very different career when the war ended. He set up a series of homes to look after people whose illnesses could not be cured in a hospital. His Cheshire Foundation homes spread around the world and by 1994 there were over 250 of them.

One man who helped to run the homes remembers meeting Cheshire for the first time. He gave a good description of him:

'I'd expected someone forceful and overpowering, and yet he seemed so ordinary. But he can command respect, loyalty, even obedience, with a quiet, unassuming authority. He gets people to do what he wants.'

Leonard Cheshire (second from the left) inspects building work being carried out on one of his homes for the sick and the elderly.

DATE CHART

1917
7 September: Cheshire is born in England.

1943
October: appointed to command 617 Squadron.

1945
9 August: watches the atomic bomb raid on Nagasaki.

1948
Begins charitable work to relieve suffering.

1981
Awarded the Order of Merit for his work in helping others.

1992
Leonard Cheshire dies.

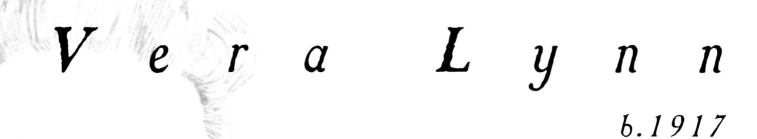

Vera Lynn

b.1917

*'The bulk of requests sent in by the members of the Eighth Army to the BBC's Overseas Service are for **sentimental** tunes by Miss Vera Lynn.'*

During the Second World War, Vera Lynn became the favourite singer of the British soldiers, sailors and pilots who were fighting all around the world. Her songs were broadcast over the radio to the troops, and she became so popular that she was called the 'Forces' Sweetheart'.

Born and brought up in London's East End, Lynn began singing as a teenager and soon found jobs with some of the leading dance bands of the day. By 1939 she was performing with the popular Ambrose Orchestra, but because of the war it was broken up.

Vera Lynn sings to troops at a concert in Britain during 1940. The people of Britain found great comfort in her sentimental songs.

38

The cover of one of Vera Lynn's songs (above), called 'The Stars Will Remember'.

Long after the war, Vera Lynn is still remembered for her singing during the conflict. This photograph shows her with the comedian Spike Milligan in 1990. They are making the 'V for Victory' symbol that was used during the war.

Lynn carried on singing as part of ENSA (Entertainment National Services Association), an organization set up by the government to make sure that the troops could get to see and hear top entertainers. The government realized that troops abroad often felt very homesick, and if they could hear a singer they liked they would feel happier – and work and fight harder.

Vera Lynn sang sentimental songs, such as 'The White Cliffs of Dover', which were very popular. At one time she was receiving over 1,000 letters every week from the troops abroad, thanking her for her songs.

As well as singing on the radio, she travelled abroad to sing to the troops. Her longest journey overseas took her to Burma (Myanmar).

After the war she carried on with her singing career, and remains popular both with ex-soldiers who remember her from the war years and with many other people all over the world.

DATE CHART

1917
Born in East Ham, London.

1937–40
Sings with the popular Ambrose Orchestra.

1944
Travels to Burma to entertain the troops.

1945
Goes back to her old career as a popular singer.

1975
Made a Dame of the British Empire (DBE).

OTHER WARTIME ENTERTAINERS

Marlene Dietrich (1901–93) – a German actress and cabaret singer.
Betty Grable – a US actress, singer and dancer.

Violette Szabo

1921-45

'If they torture me, I wonder if I will be able to stand it. People do. I hope I will. I think I will.'

Violette Szabo wrote these lines to a friend just before going on her last secret **mission** into German-occupied France. She worked for an organization called SOE (Special Operations Executive), which sent secret agents to France. There they pretended to be ordinary French people, but really they spent their time finding out about the German army and sending the information back to Britain by radio.

Violette Szabo – a brilliant secret agent and a woman of the greatest courage.

Szabo was the daughter of an English father and a French mother. She was brought up in Britain but she could speak both English and French. When the war started she was working as a shop assistant in Brixton, London. In 1940 she met and fell in love with a soldier from the French Foreign Legion called Etienne Szabo. They got married and had a daughter called Tania.

Violette Szabo worked closely with the French Résistance, an organization devoted to the ending of the Nazi occupation of France. In this picture, Résistance members are advancing through a ruined village in France.

Etienne was sent to fight in North Africa, and sadly he was killed at the famous battle of El Alamein. When she heard the news, Szabo was determined to take an active part in the war. Because she spoke good French she was accepted on an SOE training course. She was an excellent pupil and easily passed all the very difficult tests. She was especially good with weapons and became an expert at firing the Sten **sub-machine gun**.

Soon she was ready to go on a mission. This was very dangerous, for she knew that capture would lead to her being tortured and killed by the Germans. Although she was nearly caught on two occasions, her first mission to France was a great success. She discovered valuable details of German troop movements.

Supplied with weapons from SOE, French Résistance members relax during a break in their campaign against the Nazis.

Szabo's next mission ended in disaster. She parachuted into France without being spotted, but a few days later she was travelling with another agent when they were chased by a German patrol. Szabo knew her companion had vital information, and so she ordered him to run away while she held up the Germans with her Sten gun. Although she was hit by a German bullet, she carried on firing until her ammunition ran out. The German officer who captured Szabo said to her:

'I like your spirit. You put up a wonderful fight – right up until the end.'

When she refused to answer the Germans' questions she was taken to the dreaded **Gestapo** headquarters in Paris. There she was brutally tortured, but still she refused to talk. Eventually, the Gestapo gave up and sent her to a concentration camp in Germany.

On the long train journey to the camp, Szabo was chained up with other captured agents. When the train was attacked by British fighter planes, and the Nazi guards left the train to fire anti-aircraft guns, she had a chance to help the male prisoners who had been locked up without water and were dying of thirst. She passed jugs of water through the bars.

Szabo was taken to the terrible Ravensbruck concentration camp where she was forced to labour from dawn until dusk, working in the fields, cutting down trees or building roads. Her spirit was never broken, despite brutal treatment from the guards, and twice she escaped but was recaptured each time.

Eventually, the Germans decided to kill her, and Szabo and two other agents were taken to a pit and shot in the back of the head.

DATE CHART

1921
26 June: born in France as Violette Bushell.

1940
Marries Etienne Szabo, an officer in the French Foreign Legion.

1944
June: British and US troops invade German-occupied France.

1944
October: captured by German soldiers in France.

1945
Murdered at Ravensbruck concentration camp.

42

A still from the film of Violette Szabo's life, called *Carve Her Name With Pride*. The film recreates the terrible conditions at Ravensbruck concentration camp.

At his trial after the war, one of the German guards admitted that:

'All three were very brave and I was deeply moved.'

For her bravery, Violette Szabo was awarded the **George Cross** after her death – the first woman ever to receive this award.

Violette Szabo's daughter, Tania, looks at the George Cross medal awarded to her mother after she was murdered at Ravensbruck concentration camp.

OTHER SOE AGENTS

Wing Commander F. F. Yeo-Thomas
Odette Sansom
Christine Granville

Glossary

Allied forces/Allies   The 49 countries which joined together to fight Germany, Italy and Japan.

Atomic bomb   An extremely powerful bomb.

Barrage balloons   Large, fixed balloons, which were used to prevent attacks from aircraft.

Bribe   A secret gift to persuade a person to do something illegal.

Chief of Staff   The senior officer of one of the services in the armed forces.

Concentration camps   Guarded prison camps. Conditions in the Nazi camps were appalling.

Conservative Party   A British right-wing political party.

D-Day   6 June 1944, the day on which the Allied invasion of Europe began.

Dictator   A ruler who does not follow the traditional laws of government of a country but makes new rules to suit him or herself. A country ruled by a dictator is called a dictatorship.

General election   When the people of a country or state vote to choose their government.

George Cross   A British award for bravery.

Gestapo   The secret state police in Nazi Germany, which used very brutal methods.

Industrialists   People who own or control factories or other parts of a country's industry.

Mission   When a person is sent to a different country or place by a group or organization.

Morale   The level of confidence of a person or group of people.

NATO   The North Atlantic Treaty Organization, an organization set up in 1949 to defend Europe and the USA against the Soviet Union.

Nazi Germany   Germany under the rule of the Nazi Party led by Adolf Hitler, 1933–45.

Nuremberg trials   The trials of the former Nazi leaders in 1945–6, for their war crimes.

Occupied Europe   The areas of Europe that were taken over by the Nazis during the war.

Pearl Harbor   A US naval base in Hawaii, attacked by the Japanese in 1941.

Persecute   To hunt down and harm a person or group of people.

Physics   The branch of science which deals with such aspects of objects as heat, light and sound.

Right-wing   Not liking big or sudden changes or reforms.

Satirist   A writer or artist whose work contains a lot of sarcasm or mocks respected people or ideas.

Sentimental   With a lot of feeling and emotion.

Slave labour   Making a person or people work hard for no money.

Solo   Alone.

Soviet Union (or USSR)   The federation of Russian states set up by Lenin in 1922. It was broken up after a revolution in 1991.

Squadron   A basic military unit with a small number of people.

Sub-machine gun   A light, portable gun.

Supreme Allied Commander   The military officer who had control over all the Allied forces.

Surrender   When one side in a war gives up to the other.

Traitor   A person who betrays his or her country.

War effort   The work done by everyone in a country to end a war.

Books to read

General
Chambers British Biographies of the 20th Century, ed. Min Lee
  (Chambers Harrap, 1993)
Era of the Second World War series (Wayland)
Macmillan Dictionary of Biography, eds. Barry Jones and M V
  Dixon (Papermac, 1989)
Macmillan Dictionary of Women's Biography, ed. Jennifer Uglow
  (Macmillan, 1989)

Churchill
R G Grant, *Winston Churchill* (Bison, 1989)
Stewart Ross, *Churchill and the Second World War*
  (Wayland, 1987)
Brian Williams, *Winston Churchill* (Cherrytree, 1988)

Knight
A Sproule, *Women and the Arts* (Wayland, 1989)

Einstein
Nigel Calder, *Einstein's Universe* (Penguin, 1990)

Hitler
Johannes Steinhoff, Peter Pechel, Dennis Showalter, *Voices from the
  Third Reich* (Grafton, 1991)

Eisenhower
Douglas Kinnard, *Dwight D. Eisenhower: A Pictorial History*
  (Brasey's Defence Publishers, 1990)

Low
Mark Bryant, *World War II in Cartoons* (W H Smith/Bison, 1989)

Johnson
Tim Wood, *Air Travel* (Wayland, 1991)

Schindler
Thomas Kenneally, *Schindler's Ark* (Hodder, 1982, reprinted 1994)

Cheshire
Norman Moss, 'The Mystery of Cheshire VC' in the *Telegraph
  Magazine*, 24 March 1990

Lynn/Szabo
Fiona Reynoldson, *Women's War* (Wayland, 1991)

Places to visit

Churchill
Cabinet War Rooms, Clive Steps, King Charles Street,
  London SW1A 2AQ. Tel: 0171 930 6961
  The nerve centre of the wartime government.
Chartwell House, Kent (Churchill's family home).

Knight
Imperial War Museum, Lambeth Road, London SE1 6HZ.
  Tel: 0171 416 5000
  Much of her wartime work.
Tate Gallery, Millbank, London SW1. Tel: 0171 821 1313

Einstein
The Science Museum, Exhibition Road, London SW7.
  Tel: 0171 589 3456

Hitler
Imperial War Museum (as above).

Eisenhower
Imperial War Museum (as above).
D-Day Museum, Clarence Esplanade, Southsea PO5 3NT.
  Tel: 01705 827261

Low
Imperial War Museum (as above).

Johnson
The Science Museum (as above).
  General exhibits on early aviation.
Duxford Airfield, Duxford, Cambridge CB2 4QR.
  Tel: 01223 835000
  Has an Airspeed Oxford, the type of plane used on her last flight.

Schindler
Imperial War Museum (as above).

Leonard Cheshire
RAF Museum, Grahame Park Way, Hendon, London NW9 5LL.
  Tel: 0181 206 2266
Duxford Airfield and the Imperial War Museum (as above).

Vera Lynn
Imperial War Museum (as above).

Violette Szabo
Imperial War Museum (as above).

I n d e x